VICTORY

A 31 Day Devotional Guide For Women

DIANE WASHINGTON

DIANE WASHINGTON

Victory

31 DAY DEVOTIONAL GUIDE FOR WOMEN

VICTORY: 31 DAY DEVOTIONAL GUIDE FOR WOMEN
Copyright © 2016
Diane Washington

Printed in the United States of America

Library of Congress – Catalogued in Publication Data

ISBN 13: 978-0692741283
ISBN-10: 0692741283

Published by:
Jabez Books Writers' Agency
(A Division of Clark's Consultant Group)
www.clarksconsultantgroup.com

Unless otherwise indicated all scriptural quotations are taken from the King James Version of the Bible.

All rights reserved. No part of this book may be reproduced, stored in a retrieval system, or transmitted in any form or by any means, electronic, mechanical photocopying, recording, or otherwise, without written consent of the publisher except in the case of brief quotations in critical articles or reviews.

Are you willing?

Where will I find a vessel worthy, unstained, that I may fill with myself? Where among men is there one free of sin and blameless in the father's sight? How long will I search?

Will you, "my chosen one", pay the price? The way is hard and had much toil. There's no quitting, once you have committed your spirit, soul, and body that I may do with you as I choose.

Many say yes, lord. But after a season, they fall aside on the rocks, looking for rest. They seem weary even after a little while.

Oh, I've found a soul! She seems overlooked by those who are exalted above their measure. She's not even noticed by some. My, what a pure heart she has! I believe she'll make it.

Daughter! This is the Father calling you. My daughter, you have found favour in the father's eyes. I see that humility. Much boldness have I to give to you. I see the compassion that I can use to turn the water into wine, so those who are thirsty might drink from your fountain.

You seem so afraid to speak my word boldly, but it is my spirit that will consume you, so that you will stand before pious religious leaders and speak my truths that shall set men free.

My daughter, favour you have found in the eyes of God. Rejoice, for from you will I pour forth the prayers that shall turn a nation around, bringing forth fruits for my harvest.

Yet, there is a price. Only if you depend on my strength, my word, and my grace, can you pay the prices. Only in my presence will my power be sufficient for the service that I have called you to do. Your garments have to be cleaned daily, your strength renewed hour after hour.

There shall be tears, pain, travail, and much weariness as you come to this place. Not much time for the other things in this life. But I tell you this my daughter, the crown that is being made of diamonds, rubies, and gold, that the father shall give you in return for giving yourself is only a small reward for the servant who says, "Yes, Father, I hear you and I am willing".

Dedicated to my friend Eva Moore, who gave me this poem from the Lord in 1988.

TABLE OF CONTENTS

Day 1: Today is my "Obedience Day"....................11
Day 2: Today is my "Restoration of Blessings".......17 Day
Day 3: Today is my "Secret Place" Day...................23
Day 4: Today is my "Faithfulness Day"..................29
Day 5: Today is my "Forgiving Others" Day..........35
Day 6: Today is my "Thinking On The Right..........41 Thing" Day
Day 7: Today is my "Put God First Day"................47
Day 8: Today is my "More Than Enough Day"........53
Day 9: Today is my "Go For It Day".......................59
Day 10: Today is my "Reaping Blessings" Day..........65
Day 11: Today is my "Harvest Time" Day................71
Day 12: Today is my "Confidence In Him" Day.........77
Day 13: Today is my "Family" Day............................83
Day 14: Today is my "Confession" Day.....................89
Day 15: Today is my "Speak Life" Day......................95
Day 16: Today is my "Positive Attitude" Day..........101
Day 17: Today is my "Having Strength in the..........107 Lord" Day

Day 18: Today is my "Being A Wise Builder"..........113 Day

Day 19: Today is my "Learning How to Profit".......119 Day

Day 20: Today is my "Mercy" Day…………………..125

Day 21: Today is my "Seeing New Things" Day……131

Day 22: Today is my "Fearless" Day…………………137

Day 23: Today is my "Increase" Day…………………143

Day 24: Today is my "Turning It Over To God"…….149 Day

Day 25: Today is my "Sowing A Seed" Day………….155

Day 26: Today is my "Shopping For Blessings"…….161 Day

Day 27: Today is my "I Can Make It" Day……………167

Day 28: Today is my "God is the Potter And I……...173 Am The Clay Day

Day 29: Today is my "Warfare" Day…………………179

Day 30: Today is my "Celebrate My Blessed………..185 Life" Day

Day 31: Today is my "Victory" Day…………………..191

DEVOTIONAL DAY

1

TODAY IS MY "OBEDIENCE" DAY

I will set my heart toward your heart, Lord, to obey you hourly.

I will learn to:

- Keep my mouth silent when evil thoughts are present.
- Be slow to answer, quick to listen.
- Speak a kind word to everyone
- Build up any person who comes my way today
- Find something good to say, or say nothing at all.

Use these guidelines to determine how you will respond:
- Everything I do as unto the Lord
- Obedience is better than sacrifice
- Will it glorify the Lord?

If what I want to say doesn't meet all three of these guidelines, then I will not speak those words.

Choose to love the Lord your God and to obey Him and to cling to Him, for He is your life and the length of your days.

Deuteronomy 30:20

Prayer FOR TODAY

Lord, I choose to set my heart toward you, seek your face and hear your voice today that I might obey you in all things.

Amen

Future Bible Study:
Deuteronomy 28; 29:1-29; 30:14-16
Romans 6:16
2 Corinthians 10:5

Personal Notes:

DEVOTIONAL DAY

2

TODAY IS MY "RESTORATION OF BLESSINGS" DAY

For every seed that the devil takes, God will restore it back again.

- The devil must return seven times what he has taken.

- God will restore the years that the canker worms have eaten up.

- God can bring life to every dead situation in your life because He has resurrection power to bring life.

And I will restore to you the years that the locust hath eaten, the cankerworm, and the caterpiller, and the palmerworm, my great army which I sent among you.

Joel 2:25

Prayer
FOR TODAY

I speak life to every dead situation in my life. Bring resurrection power to create a new me, in Jesus' Name I pray.

Amen

Future Bible Study:
Mark 16:6-18
Luke 5:1-7
Exodus 22:4
Deuteronomy 22:2
Jeremiah 27:22; 30:17

Personal Notes:

_____

_____

_____

_____

_____

_____

_____

_____

_____

DEVOTIONAL DAY

3

TODAY IS MY "SECRET PLACE" DAY

Get into your prayer closet to talk with God.

- Call upon Him in your day of trouble and He will direct your path.

- Believe that He will hear you and be near you.

- When you are in your secret place, use the power that His word gives you to move the mountains in your life.

Remember:
1. There is no pace that God cannot go
2. There isn't a need too big for Him, that He can't fulfill
3. God answers all of His children who call upon Him.
4. There isn't a time too late for Him to come through for you.

In your secret place God will answer your requests. Set a time to be alone with God in prayer. Say to that mountain – "Move mountain! Mountain get out of my way!"

But thou, when thou prayest, enter into thy closet, and when thou hast shut thy door, pray to thy Father which is in secret; and thy Father which seeth in secret shall reward thee openly.

Matthew 6:6

Prayer FOR TODAY

Lord, I will pray without ceasing because you are there for me at all times. You hear my cry and deliver me from the enemy's hand. Help me today to be more sensitive to my secret place with you.

Amen

Future Bible Study:
Deuteronomy 30:14; 29:29
Romans 10:14-20

Personal Notes:

DEVOTIONAL DAY

4

TODAY IS MY "FAITHFULNESS" DAY

God is always faithful even when you are not.

- His blessings are new every morning. Great is His faithfulness.

- When nothing seems right, God will stretch out His hands to help me.

- Faithful is my God, unto faithful people.

- He looks to me to be faithful in all my house (desire) and needs and He will open up the flow living water to me.

Know therefore that the LORD your God is God, the faithful God who keeps covenant and steadfast love with those who love him and keep his commandments, to a thousand generations.

Deuteronomy 7:9

Prayer
FOR TODAY

Our Father, I know that you are faithful in all of your promises to me. Help me today to be faithful in all my house and to do all as though it was unto you. Oh Lord, my God, today and always.

                                      Amen

Future Bible Study:
Psalms 31:38; 99:9; 145:19; 128:1-6; 146
Proverbs 14:5
Deuteronomy. 22:14
Nehemiah 9:8

Personal Notes:

DEVOTIONAL DAY

5

TODAY IS MY "FORGIVING OTHERS" DAY

Good and merciful is my God.

- Unforgiveness stops the flow of my blessings. It ties the hand of God to return good things to an unforgiving person.

- Through unforgiveness comes:
    1. Sickness
    2. Obsession
    3. Depression
    4. Confusion

- But confusion can wash away all – bring forgiveness.

- Unforgiveness is bad seed. Forgiveness is good seed.

- Thrust forth to your future blessings.

- I must choose to forgive those who have hurt you, in order to release God's flow of blessings into your life.

For if ye forgive men their trespasses, your heavenly Father will also forgive you.

Matthew 6:14

Prayer FOR TODAY

Today I will forgive, and praise Him for all good things. I set my will to forgive anyone, today and forever, who has abused my trust or who has hurt me in any way. I have a heart to forgive because I choose to receive from God.

Amen

Future Bible Study:
Psalms 32; 86:5-17; 103:3-22
Matthew 19:21-35
Mark 11:25
Colossians 3:13

Personal Notes:

DEVOTIONAL DAY

6

TODAY IS MY "THINKING ON THE RIGHT THING" DAY

Whatsoever things are pure and of good report I should think on.

- Think on These things:
    1. Is it True?
    2. Is it Kind?
    3. Is it Necessary?

- I should check on these things before you speak:
    1. Everything I do as unto the Lord
    2. Obedience is better than sacrifice
    3. Will it glorify God?

- My words have power to bring life or death.

"Now unto him that is able to do exceedingly abundantly above all that we ask or think, according to the power that worketh in us."

Ephesians 3:20

Prayer
FOR TODAY

Lord, be a watchman over my mouth and actions that I may not sin against you in all that I say and all that I do.

Amen

Future Bible Study:
James 3:1-18
Psalm 32:9
1 Corinthians 2:6
Romans 12:9
Proverbs 11:18

Personal Notes:

DEVOTIONAL DAY

7

TODAY IS MY "PUT GOD FIRST" DAY

Putting God first means trusting Him in all situation in your life.

When you are confident in His care, you don't worry about anything.

Just place your troubles In His care, where there is no despair.

<u>My goal</u>
My main goal is to be one with God and love him with all my heart (make him your obsession).

- Why do I need to put God first?
    1. Because He is God (I am that I am)
    2. Because He is a personal God
    3. Because of what He did for me (Calvary was for ME)
    4. Because wise men call out to Him.

- Our creator stands still for us whenever we cry out to him. He is ready, willing, and able to help us with all our needs.

Trust in the LORD with all thine heart; and lean not unto thine own understanding.

Proverbs 3:15

Prayer
FOR TODAY

Lord, help me choose to put you first each day. You are my light, and my strength for today, and I know that you put me first each day.

                                                  Amen

Future Bible Study:
Exodus 20:2-3; 3:14
Matthew 9
Luke 18:35
Acts 2:1-47

Personal Notes:

_____

_____

_____

_____

_____

_____

_____

_____

_____

_____

DEVOTIONAL DAY

8

TODAY IS MY "MORE THAN ENOUGH" DAY

God is a great God! He has more than enough for me.

- He can supply more than we can ever use or will need today, tomorrow, or forever.

- There is no lack in my life, only the opportunity to sow another seed to reap another harvest.

- What I have, place in His hand. He will multiply it a thousand times over.

- A grain of corn is one seed which brings forth one stalk- but God brings many ears of corn from that one stalk. God will do the same thing for me, if I learn to sow with Him.

*I have been young,
and now am old; yet have I
not seen the righteous
forsaken, nor his seed
begging bread.*

Psalm 37:25

Prayer FOR TODAY

There is no need so great that you, Lord, cannot meet that need. Help me to see you meeting my needs today and always. A miracle was needed, so you created a miracle for me today. Thank you, Lord.

                                                 Amen

Future Bible Study:
Exodus 36:5-7
Deuteronomy 11:7-27; 28
Job 36:11

Personal Notes:

DEVOTIONAL DAY

9

TODAY IS MY "GO FOR IT" DAY

The blessing is for my asking

- There are many blessings waiting to be delivered to your door. Ten thousand blessings has He to give freely to you.

- Faith in the name of Jesus brings blessings.

- Ten spies went out into the land. Two were wise, but five couldn't see (spiritually blind). Only five could catch the vision of the land.

- Go for it! Take the land; the promise is true! You are well able to possess anything with the word of the Lord!

- The harvest time is now. Your season has arrived!

- Go for it! Catch your vision!

And whatsoever ye shall ask in my name, that will I do, that the Father may be glorified in the Son.

John 14:13

Prayer
FOR TODAY

Lord, help me to see the Promised Land. Keep the promise before me and the pit behind me. Father God, every day brings a life changing situation. Help me to see the rainbow after the storms in my life today.

                                              Amen

Future Bible Study:
Numbers 13
Mark 9:23
Judges 18:2-17
Genesis 42:9-34
Joshua 2:1-21

Personal Notes:

DEVOTIONAL DAY

10

TODAY IS MY "REAPING BLESSINGS" DAY

If I sow in hourly, God will sow hourly blessings.

- Don't make a vow that you are not willing to keep.

- Vows are the act of making a covenant with a person (in this case God).

- Some vows I might make to God:
    1. To be faithful to Him
    2. To be obedient to Him
    3. To be committed to Him and focused on Him
    4. To be united with Him
    5. To be loyal to Him

- It is better to never make a vow to God then to make a vow and break that vow!

Better is it that thou shouldest not vow, than that thou shouldest vow and not pay.

Ecclesiastes 5:5

Prayer
FOR TODAY

Oh Father, I want to commit my life to walk as you walk, to see as you see, and to do as you do. In order to bring about the blessings you want in my life. I commit myself to you. I know that I can reap blessings by the vows that I keep, the seeds that I plant, and the words that I speak.

         Amen

Future Bible Study:
Isaiah 54:9
Isaiah 55:11
Matthew 26:63

Personal Notes:

DEVOTIONAL DAY

11

TODAY IS MY "HARVEST TIME" DAY

Seed time brings harvest time into your life

- There is a season to sow and a season to harvest all the seeds I have planted.

- Harvest time is when I set my faith unto God who has more than enough for me.

- There is never any lack in any father's house.

- The riches of the sinners are laid up for the righteous.

- The seed I have planted will yield good fruit.

Cast thy bread upon the waters: for thou shalt find it after many days.

Ecclesiastes 11:1

Prayer
FOR TODAY

Father God, I thank you today for being my provider and giving me the promise of the harvest today. Great is our God and mighty is His reward.

Amen

Future Bible Study:
Malachi 3:10
Matt 25:14-29

Personal Notes:

DEVOTIONAL DAY

12

TODAY IS MY "CONFIDENCE IN HIM" DAY

My confidence in God will move the mountains in my life.

- I'm in Him and my confidence is in Him, so I will not fail.

- I'm built up with my confidence in God.

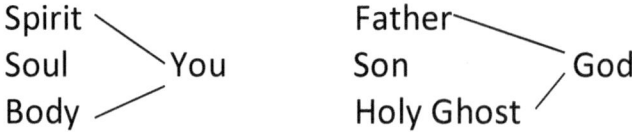

- God has enough power to handle any problem you may encounter.

And this is the confidence that we have in him, that, if we ask any thing according to his will, he heareth us.

I John 5:14

Prayer
FOR TODAY

Lord, my confidence is in you, to take me anywhere you want. Do whatever you will with my life. I place my life in your hands because I'm sure you will be able to take me through any situation!

        Amen

Future Bible Study:
Romans 6:16
Mark 11:24
Psalms 27:1-5
2 Corinthians 12:9-10

Personal Notes:

DEVOTIONAL DAY

13

TODAY IS MY "FAMILY" DAY

A family is one of God's greatest blessings

- Children who have been built well will, in turn, become good child builders themselves.

- God does the building, but HE allows parents to be the overseer of the building.

- Parents should always put their children's spiritual training first- no matter what.

- No matter what my child looks like now, there can be a change from inside that will change the outside.

- If I don't walk in the Word in my home, if I don't teach the Word, and if I don't practice the Word- I will not have a spirit-filled home with God's abundant blessings.

*Lo, children are
an heritage of the LORD:
and the fruit of the womb
is his reward.*

Psalm 127:3

Prayer

FOR TODAY

Lord, I will lift up your name to my family and teach you words to my children. Today, I will put you first in everything and give you the glory for the work done in my family.

Amen

Future Bible Study:
Psalms 127:1-2
Deuteronomy 11:18,21
Colossians 3:14

Personal Notes:

DEVOTIONAL DAY

14

TODAY IS MY "CONFESSION" DAY

Jesus Christ is Lord over your life

- I must confess all of my sins before Him.

- What I am in Christ – I am a child of the king. I am in the royal priesthood.

- Where I am in Christ – I am an overcomer

- What I possess in Christ – I have authority and power over my enemies.

- When Jesus is the Lord of my life, He reigns over all situations that come into my life.

- God is more than enough for all of my needs.

- Acknowledge that God rules over my life.

That if thou shalt confess with thy mouth the Lord Jesus, and shalt believe in thine heart that God hath raised him from the dead, thou shalt be saved.

Romans 10:9

Prayer
FOR TODAY

I acknowledge you, oh God, and confess you before men, in my daily communion at home, on my way out and on my way in. When I rise and when I lay down, I will confess you as Lord over all creation, ruler of the universe, controller of my heart today and forever more.

                                                  Amen

Future Bible Study:
Psalms 32:5
Proverbs 28:13
Ezra 10:11
Romans 10:10
1 Timothy 6:13

Personal Notes:

DEVOTIONAL DAY

15

TODAY IS MY "SPEAK LIFE" DAY

I will speak life into all the dead situations in my life.

- There is life in the power of the tongue.

- Create life giving words for your bad situations:

    a) There are blessings coming your way.
    b) When Satan gets to messing – God gets to blessing.
    c) There is a fruitful season in life – everything you touch has life.

*Death and life
are in the power of the
tongue: and they
that love it shall eat the
fruit thereof.*

Proverbs 18:21

Prayer
FOR TODAY

Father, in the name of Jesus, give me the power to create wealth and health in my life. For greater is He who is in me than he who is in the world. God, grant me power in my weakness.

Amen

Future Bible Study:
Ephesians 1:19
Colossians 1:29
1 Corinthians 15:10

Personal Notes:

DEVOTIONAL DAY

16

TODAY IS MY "POSITIVE ATTITUDE" DAY

My attitude determines my walk with Him.

- If I keep my eyes focused on Jesus, I can change any circumstances.

- My attitude will bring transformation to a dead situation.

- You were put here to attached Satan, not to have him attack you!

- I will walk through fire and come out as pure as gold.

- I will live and breathe flesh to dry bones and they will live again.

- Acknowledge that God rules over your life.

*I can do
all things through
Christ which
strengtheneth me.*

Philippians 4:13

Prayer FOR TODAY

God, I know sometimes it is you shaking my life. I pray that I will always learn from this shaking. But when it is the enemy of my soul, I will rise up above that will strength from your Holy Spirit.

                                                Amen

Future Bible Study:
Proverbs 4:23
Genesis 13:17
Psalms 103:20
Matthew 20:25
Hebrews 10:22; 10:35-36

Personal Notes:

DEVOTIONAL DAY

17

TODAY IS MY "HAVING STRENGTH IN THE LORD" DAY

You will stay in perfect peace because your mind is on Jesus.

- Jesus is present help in time of trouble, His right hand will uphold me.

- Strengthening my brethren often will strengthen me.

- Let the weak say "I'm strong" and let the strong say "I'm weak", for what the Lord has done for me.

*I have set the L*ORD *always before me: because he is at my right hand, I shall not be moved.*

Psalm 16:8

Prayer FOR TODAY

Lord, I know you are my strength when there is no hope, joy or peace left within me. That you cause me to triumph over my enemies and cause me to have victory over any situations in my life. Teach me, Lord, to lean more on your strength than my own.

                                                Amen

Future Bible Study:
Isaiah 26:3-4; 27:5; 40:21-31; 41:10; 46
Job 22:21

Personal Notes:

DEVOTIONAL DAY

18

TODAY IS MY "BEING A WISE BUILDER" DAY

For every wise woman builds her house upon the wisdom of the Lord.

- Say unto wisdom, thou art my sister: and call understanding thy kinswoman.

- Give instructions to a wise woman, and she will be yet wiser.

- Show yourself a pattern of good works.

- Speak words, sweet as a honeycomb, that you pleasing to the ear.

- Self-control will be before you at all times.

- Women always control the tone of their household.

*She openeth her
mouth with wisdom; and
in her tongue is the
law of kindness.*

Proverbs 31:26

Prayer
FOR TODAY

Lord, my Father, teach me to be a wiser builder, to give my life a firm foundation. To build up my husband and children. To see beyond their faults and see their needs. Teach me to know when to speak and when to pray. Let me be slow to anger and quick to love. To understand and lend a hand, when one is needed. Build me to be a wiser woman, oh Lord.

                                                                   Amen

---

Future Bible Study:
Proverbs 7:4; 9:9; 9:13, 18; 13:2; 14
Titus 2:3, 5
Psalms 84:5

Personal Notes:

DEVOTIONAL DAY

19

TODAY IS MY "LEARNING HOW TO PROFIT" DAY

I shall profit in whatever I do. Because I do all things unto God.

- I will profit because my Father possesses all things – the cattle on a thousand hills.

- God is the master planner for my life.

- He brings me to the place of increase.

- I can enjoy increase because it's my Father's pleasure to give me the kingdom.

- I am only one step away from seeds that I plant, to harvest for me.

The LORD shall command the blessing upon thee in thy storehouses, and in all that thou settest thine hand unto; and he shall bless thee in the land which the LORD thy God giveth thee.

Proverbs 28:8

Prayer FOR TODAY

Father, in the name of Jesus, I praise you because you own the cattle on a thousand hills and you teach me how to be successful. Father, I lay hold of your word and activate your plans for my life today. Teach me how to profit in all things, Lord. In Jesus' Name I pray.

                                                  Amen

Future Bible Study:
1 Corinthians 10:33
James 2:14
Proverbs 13:22; 12:2, 3
Titus 3:8
Psalms 37:26
Genesis 47:34

Personal Notes:

DEVOTIONAL DAY

20

TODAY IS MY "MERCY" DAY

For the Lord is good, His mercy endures forever.

- My Lord is merciful and gracious to me.

- He never forgets who I am, and He always renders a hand.

- I can't stop His mercy from flowing nor can I stop His blessings from showing.

- Mercy rewrote my life.

- Jesus reshaped my style.

- The Holy Spirit renewed my mind.

- And friends help me survive!

Have mercy upon me, O God, according to thy lovingkindness: according unto the multitude of thy tender mercies blot out my transgressions.

Psalm 51:1

Prayer
FOR TODAY

No matter what I do, Lord, You are there to pick me up. You wipe my mistakes away. Help me to show mercy to my fellow man today; to see their needs through love filled- eyes.

Amen.

Future Bible Study:
Psalms 100
Jer. 33:11
Romans 9:15-23
Matthew 15:22; 23:23

Personal Notes:

DEVOTIONAL DAY 21

TODAY IS MY "SEEING NEW THINGS" DAY

New beginnings start when I believe, through my faith, in God.

- A new heart and a new spirit for the Lord is my desire.

- Old things are passed away when I received the newness that God is doing in my life.

- The Lord will wash away all of the old man in me. Resurrect the new man so that I can walk into obedience with him.

- All the promises in God's book are mine- every scripture, verse, and line will spring forth divine.

- My thoughts should be pure in order to attract the blessings that are sure to be mine.

Remember ye not the former things, neither consider the things of old. Behold, I will do a new thing; now it shall spring forth; shall ye not know it? I will even make a way in the wilderness, and rivers in the desert.

Isaiah 43:18-19

Prayer
FOR TODAY

Father, my desire is to be that overcoming woman of God that you want me to be. To live a victorious life through you. To become the wife, mother, daughter, sister, friend, that you want me to be. Place a new mind, heart, and spirit within me today I pray.

                                        Amen

Future Bible Study:
Isaiah 1:19; 42:9-10; 43:18, 21; 65:17
Ezekiel 36:16, 29
Exodus 17:6
Revelation 21:5

Personal Notes:

DEVOTIONAL DAY 22

TODAY IS MY "FEARLESS" DAY

Fear not because my Father is well able to handle any problem.

- Fear is under my feet – faith is in my heart.

- There is not any fear that Christ cannot erase out of my life.

- Fear is my faith turned upside down. Faith is fear on the run. I can overcome every fear in my life through Jesus Christ.

- I can rise up with faith every time fear tries to enter into my life.

- Fear of the Lord is the beginning of wisdom.

*For God has not
given us a spirit of fear, but
of power and of love and
of a sound mind.*

I Timothy 1:7

Prayer FOR TODAY

Father, I know you haven't given me the spirit of fear, but one of peace and sound mind. Because you have recreated my thought patterns and because fear has no part of me now, fear is on the run. Faith has taken control and has full power.

Amen

Future Bible Study:
Isaiah 10, 13, 14; 35:10; 43:5
Jeremiah 30:10; 35:10
Deuteronomy 1:29; 31:6
Job 25:2; 11:15

Personal Notes:

DEVOTIONAL DAY

23

TODAY IS MY "INCREASE" DAY

I believe God for the increase in my life.

- The increase comes when I believe God for the harvest.

- I sow the seed, Heaven waters it, but God gives the increase.

- When I place my needs in God's hands, I release his blessings plan.

- "Sow – I'll bless you and multiply your harvest over and over again," says the Lord.

*Riches and honour
are with me; yea, durable
riches and righteousness.*

Proverbs 8:18

Prayer
FOR TODAY

Father, in the name of Jesus, I believe you for the increase in my life. I believe that you will multiply more into my account. I sow, heaven waters, but I know you will bring the abundant increase into my life.

Amen

Future Bible Study:
Hebrews 2:1
Deuteronomy 7:13
Luke 26:4
Galatians 6:19
Psalms 68:19

Personal Notes:

DEVOTIONAL DAY

24

TODAY IS MY "TURN IT OVER TO GOD" DAY

I can loosen the burdens that so easily beset me.

- The burden I have today can be carried another way. Jesus can carry every burden better than I can.

- The choice is mine to give it up to God or to struggle with it.

- My problem is solved when I choose to turn it over to the Master's hand.

- My seed of faith goes ahead to make certain of my life ahead.

- There is not a seed that leaves my hand that God can't command to bring forth a blessings for me.

- I can choose to give it all to God and walk free again.

*Cast thy burden
upon the LORD, and he shall
sustain thee: he shall never
suffer the righteous
to be moved.*

Psalm 55:11

Prayer

FOR TODAY

Today, Lord, I choose to turn over all my problems to you and receive your out-pouring of blessings and mercy for my life. I can't do anything of myself but I can be victorious through every problem with you by my side.

Amen

Future Bible Study:
Psalms 111:1
Revelation 22:7

Personal Notes:

DEVOTIONAL DAY

25

TODAY IS MY "SOWING A SEED" DAY

Each seed I sow is for my future ahead.

- I sow today for tomorrow's blessings.

- Reaper is sower, and sower is reaper.

- Abundance is from my obedience to God.

- There's not a seed of mine that doesn't sprout, to reap a fruitful harvest.

- If I want love – I must sow it.

- If I want joy – I must sow joy into the lives of others.

- If I want finances – I must sow my finances into the Lord's work.

- Whatever I want or need in life, I must sow it in order to reap the harvest.

- A miracle is only a seed sowed away to reap the miracle have need of today.

*Be not deceived;
God is not mocked: for
whatsoever a man soweth,
that shall he also reap.*

Galatians 6:7

Prayer FOR TODAY

Father, I'm a sower and a reaper, because you give me power to reap in any harvest that I plant. I will sow my seed each day – to reap a harvest today and every day.

Amen

Future Bible Study:
Proverbs 13:22
Malachi 3:10
Matthew 13:4
Ephesians 6:8
Isaiah 48:17

Personal Notes:

DEVOTIONAL DAY

26

TODAY IS MY "SHOPPING FOR BLESSINGS" DAY

Shopping comes from the Lord to bring the blessings into my life.

- There is a season for my trouble to bring about a season for my blessings.

- After the storm comes the rainbow.

- There is a season and a reason for shopping from God and there is always a blessing after a fall.

- God is a molder and I am the clay – a potter who is waiting for the finished perfection of clay.

- Shopping comes from God, to bring about the blessings in my life.

*To every thing
there is a season, and a
time to every purpose
under the heaven.*

Ecclesiastes 3:1

Prayer
FOR TODAY

Lord, I know when you mold and shape me, it is for the blessings and growth in my life. Help me to understand the shopping and be grateful for the blessings you have for me today.

                                                  Amen

Future Bible Study:
John 15
Genesis 12:2
Psalms 5:12
Jeremiah 18
Deuteronomy 28:4-6
Proverbs 20:7

Personal Notes:

DEVOTIONAL DAY

27

TODAY IS MY "I CAN MAKE IT" DAY

This storm I am going through will not destroy me.

- I can make it, because I am going with God's strength and not my own.

- There is not a storm or mountain that God cannot control.

- God's the creator.
    1. Whatever I need – God has it.
    2. Whatever I want – God can create it.
    3. Whatever I desire – God can supply it.

- God never allows a testing without providing an escape.

- Our Father never gives a task without under girding and equipping us to perform it.

For our light affliction, which is but for a moment, worketh for us a far more exceeding [and] eternal weight of glory.

2 Corinthians 4:17

Prayer
FOR TODAY

God show me just what to do through this storm today. Direct my way and reveal to me the way I should go today.

        Amen

Future Bible Study:
Philippians 4:19
Psalms 25
Romans 16:27
1 Corinthians 10:13

Personal Notes:

DEVOTIONAL DAY

28

TODAY IS MY "GOD IS THE POTTER & I AM THE CLAY" DAY

Satan comes to shake my faith but God comes to bless me abundantly.

- Mold my life and shape my tongue.

- If I learn to control my tongue, I will have half of all my problems solved.

- An obedient life brings about three things in my life.

    1) Shaping – mold the life
    2) Making – breaking the will of my life
    3) Blessings – come forth in my life

Therefore, my beloved brethren, be ye stedfast, unmoveable, always abounding in the work of the Lord, forasmuch as ye know that your labour is not in vain in the Lord.

1 Corinthians 15:58

Prayer
FOR TODAY

Father, God, mold and shape my life today to be whatever you want for me today, to be what you desire for my life. Mold my life and shape my life so others will see Jesus in me.

Amen

Future Bible Study:
Isaiah 64:8
Isaiah 45:12-13
Jeremiah 18:6

Personal Notes:

DEVOTIONAL DAY

29

TODAY IS MY "WARFARE" DAY

Whatever I want — give it to God.

- God can do more with a little than I can with a lot.

- Holding on to God brings about victory.

- There is war in the spirit when I pray on earth for victory over Satan.

- Warfare causes mountains to crumble; valleys turn into plains; storms to cease in my life.

For the weapons of our warfare are not carnal, but mighty through God to the pulling down of strong holds.

2 Corinthians 10:4

Prayer
FOR TODAY

Lord, I put on my spiritual armor in order to go to war against satan – to quench all his fiery darts aimed at me.

                                                Amen

Future Bible Study:
Ephesians 6:10-20
Romans 8:1

Personal Notes:

DEVOTIONAL DAY

30

TODAY IS MY "CELEBRATE MY BLESSED LIFE" DAY

God is the blessed controller of all things. All things were created by Him.

- From Him all things come and have their being:

    1. My life – breath, health
    2. My child – his life, his health
    3. My spiritual – in charity, in faith, in purity
    4. My economic life – my job, my wealth

- For every creature of God is good. Nothing will be refused, if it is received with thanksgiving.

- When you have Jesus Christ in your life you can celebrate life – because blessings and honor will be yours.

For of him, and through him, and to him, are all things: to whom be glory for ever. Amen.

Romans 11:36

Prayer FOR TODAY

Father, in the Name of Jesus, I come to my creator to be in control of my life. Let me be as great a blessing to others as you are to me.

Amen

Future Bible Study:
1 Timothy 6:15
Genesis 1:1
1 John 5:14-15
Nahum 1:7

Personal Notes:

DEVOTIONAL DAY

31

TODAY IS MY "VICTORY" DAY

You have to see yourself rise out of the pit and into the palace.

- Looking on the promise of God and remind God that you know that He knows the the promise of God Yea and Amen.

- Your needs will be met, because you trust in a Savior who can meet every dire situation in your life face to face each day – because victory is yours in Jesus Christ.

- You don't need an army when you have Jesus. Then will be too many.

- Return and regroup.

- Put praises into your mouth, joy into your heart and overcome all the trials and tribulations that satan throws at you.

- You will part your Red Sea with the word of God – warfare goes out before victory comes in.

But thanks be to God, which giveth us the victory through our Lord Jesus Christ.

I Corinthians 15:57

Prayer
FOR TODAY

Victory is mine in you, Christ Jesus. I'm looking differently and speaking differently now that I am walking closer to you. Bring your promises down to me in the name of Jesus. Lord, help me to always see the victory before the war starts.

Amen

Future Bible Study:
Deuteronomy 12:8-25
Judges 7:24
2 Chronicles 26:5
Proverbs 3:1-4
Mark 10:27

Personal Notes:

About Apostle Diane Washington

Diane McDaniel Washington is a young mother and wife, who speaks on the promises of God's Word for today. She believes in the written Word of God. She actively participates in the blessings of God throughout her Christian walk in life.

She is the wife of William Andre McDaniel, with whom she celebrates 17 years of blissful marriage. To this union were born four beautiful children – Kimberly Natasha (deceased in 1979 at age 5), Kesha Renee (9), Kemual Andrea (3) and Kristian Rejoice (2). After the traumatic death of Kimberly, Diane and Williams took inventory of their lives and received Jesus Christ as their personal savior. Their walk with Christ has been attacked repeatly by the devil; however, Diane and William remain victorious and true servants of God.

Apostle Washington is an ordinary woman that has walked closely with God over the past decade. Because her faith has been constantly tested, she can provide you with true and personal testimonies of victory over the devil.

She has served on many boards and in various organizations. Apostle Washington is a much sought after speaker on numerous subjects, such as, the Christian walk, total godly woman, marriage healing, etc. Apostle Washington faithfully and diligently volunteers her services in community outreach programs, such as FoodShare on Montgomery, United Gospel Outreach, etc.

Apostle Washington reside in Detroit, MI.

Give thanks with a grateful heart. I give thanks to my dearest family and friends:

- Evg. Mike Murdock, who gave me the inspiration to write this guide.

- My dear friend in the Lord, Eva Moore, who believed in my desire and contributed a poem for my effort.

- My mother, Elizabeth Peterson, who watched over my children so that I could pray and commune with God.

- My sister, Mimi McDaniel, who has always used her secretarial skills to assist me in all of my endeavors.

- My Friday night Bible study group (Ballock, Barbara, and Wilamae), who prayed unceasingly with and for me.

- Finally, Wayne Lawerence, who put it all together!

God bless you all and thanks again.

Dee Dee

To order more Copies, please visit:

www._____

Other Resource Tool by Apostle Diane Washington

www.ingramcontent.com/pod-product-compliance
Lightning Source LLC
Chambersburg PA
CBHW061304110426
42742CB00012BA/2049